WINSTON CHURCHILL

A BIOGRAPHY OF THE BULLDOG OF BRITAIN

ROSS DANVERS

CONTENTS

INTRODUCTION

In the annals of history, few names shine as brightly or weigh as heavily as that of Winston Churchill. A figure synonymous with indomitable spirit, razor-sharp wit, and a leadership style that navigated Britain through its darkest hours, Churchill remains a towering icon of the 20th century. "Winston Churchill: A Biography of the Bulldog of Britain" aims to provide a concise yet comprehensive exploration of the life and legacy of this remarkable individual. This unofficial biography delves into the multifaceted dimensions of Churchill's existence: from his birth into the aristocracy to his final days, capturing the essence of a man whose life story is a testament to resilience, courage, and the power of words.

Chapter 1, "Early Life and Education," sets the stage, introducing us to Churchill's ancestry, his birth at Blenheim Palace, and his formative years, which were marked by a combination of privilege and emotional neglect. We follow young Winston's journey through education, where his rebellious nature and independent thinking began to surface, foreshadowing the extraordinary path he was to embark upon.

In Chapter 2, "Military Beginnings and Adventures," we traverse the globe with Churchill, from the battlefields of Cuba to the boer war in South Africa, witnessing the making of a war correspondent and a soldier, whose experiences would deeply influence his worldview and political career.

Chapter 3, "Entry into Politics," chronicles Churchill's foray into the political arena, detailing his early political triumphs and setbacks, his shifting allegiances between political parties, and his rising prominence as a national figure.

"The Wilderness Years," detailed in Chapter 4, explores a period of political isolation and personal reflection for Churchill. It was during these years that he honed his skills as a writer and speaker, and most importantly, issued prescient warnings about the rise of Nazi Germany.

World War II, the defining chapter of Churchill's life and arguably of the 20th century, is the focus of Chapter 5. We examine his leadership through Britain's darkest days, his rallying speeches, and his role in shaping the strategies that would lead to Allied victory.

Chapter 6, "Postwar Years," and Chapter 7, "Second Premiership," cover the complexities of Churchill's later political career, including his time out of office, his return to power, and his efforts to address post-war challenges and the early stages of the Cold War.

Chapter 8, "Final Years," recounts Churchill's life after retirement, reflecting on his enduring influence and the recognition he received, culminating in his death in 1965.

In Chapter 9, "Life Outside of Politics," we explore Churchill's personal interests, his family life, and his hobbies, shedding light on the man behind the public persona.

Chapter 10, "Churchill the Author," celebrates Churchill's prolific career as a writer and historian, which earned him the Nobel Prize in Literature for his contribution to historical and biographical writing.

Finally, Chapter 11, "Winston Churchill – A Timeline," provides a succinct overview of the key events in Churchill's life, offering readers a quick reference guide to the chronology of his extraordinary journey.

"Winston Churchill: A Biography of the Bulldog of Britain" endeavors to capture the essence of a man who was not only a pivotal figure in history but also a complex human being with strengths, flaws, and a legacy that continues to inspire and provoke debate. Through the chapters of this book, readers will gain insight into Churchill's multifaceted character, his enduring impact on the world stage, and the indelible mark he left on history.

CHAPTER 1: EARLY LIFE AND EDUCATION

In the annals of history, few figures loom as large as Winston Leonard Spencer-Churchill. Born into the storied Spencer-Churchill family on November 30, 1874, his early years were marked by a blend of aristocratic privilege and personal challenges that shaped the contours of the man he would become. This chapter delves into the genesis of Churchill's journey, exploring his birth into an eminent family, his formative years filled with the rigors of education, and the early trials that forged his indomitable spirit. From the grandeur of Blenheim Palace to the disciplined halls of Harrow School and the Royal Military Academy at Sandhurst, we trace the path of a young Churchill, uncovering the experiences that nurtured his burgeoning qualities of leadership, resilience, and a lifelong appetite for adventure.

Winston was born into a family of significant historical and aristocratic standing. His lineage was not only steeped in the military and political history of Britain but was also intimately connected with the highest echelons of the British nobility. On one side, he was a direct descendant of the Duke of Marlborough, one of Britain's most illustrious military commanders, whose victories in the War of the Spanish Succession had been immortalized at Blenheim Palace, a gift from a grateful nation. This palatial estate, with its vast grounds and splendid architecture, was where Winston first opened his eyes to the world, symbolizing the weight of heritage and expectation that would mark his journey through life.

His father, Lord Randolph Churchill, was a prominent Conservative politician, serving as Secretary of State for India and Chancellor of the Exchequer. His mother, Jennie Jerome, was an American heiress, the daughter of a wealthy New York financier. This blend of British aristocracy and American entrepreneurship endowed Churchill with a unique perspective, merging the traditional with the burgeoning spirit of modernity that characterized the late 19th century.

Despite the grandeur of his birthright, Churchill's early childhood was marked by emotional distance from his parents. Lord Randolph was often engrossed in his political career, and Jennie, while loving, was absorbed in the social whirl of the aristocracy. Consequently, young Winston often found himself in the care of his beloved nanny, Elizabeth Ann Everest, who provided the emotional support and affection he craved. His early years were characterized by a quest for parental approval and attention, shaping his ambitious and determined nature.

Churchill's formal education began at St. George's School in Ascot, Berkshire, where he was enrolled at the age of seven. His time at St. George's was far from pleasant; he struggled academically and was often at odds with the school's strict disciplinary methods. Churchill's independent spirit and disdain for rote learning did not endear him to a system that prized conformity and academic rigor in traditional subjects like Latin and mathematics. This period was marred by feelings of isolation and inadequacy, as he failed to meet the expectations set by his family and schoolmasters. However, it was also during this tumultuous time that Churchill's resilience began to take shape. His difficulties in adapting to the traditional educational environment underscored his need for a different kind of learning—one that engaged his imagination and interests.

In 1888, Churchill's educational journey took a pivotal turn as he entered Harrow School. Though his entry was not into the school's most prestigious houses, due to academic performance not meeting the highest standards, Harrow would become a place where Churchill began to find his footing. Initially, he continued to struggle with subjects that did not interest him, but Harrow offered something

St. George's did not: opportunities for Churchill to explore his burgeoning interests in history, military affairs, and literature.

At Harrow, Churchill's academic performance began to improve in the areas that captivated him. He excelled in English and history, displaying a remarkable memory for historical facts and figures, as well as a talent for debate and public speaking. These subjects allowed Churchill to connect with the narratives of great men and events of the past, seeing in them the qualities he aspired to possess. His interest in military affairs was also nurtured at Harrow, where he joined the Harrow Rifle Corps, further solidifying his fascination with military strategy and leadership.

Beyond academics, Churchill's character was shaped by the challenges he faced. The loneliness and feelings of inadequacy that marked his earlier years did not vanish, but they were met with a growing resilience and determination to prove himself. It was at Harrow that Churchill began to develop a sense of his own identity and potential, driven by a desire to achieve greatness despite early setbacks.

Churchill's time at Harrow was also marked by the development of his literary talents. He became involved in the school's debating society and contributed to the Harrow School magazine, activities that honed his skills in writing and oratory. These pursuits not only provided an outlet for his creative expression but also laid the groundwork for his future career as a writer and statesman.

Following his time at Harrow, Churchill sought to attend the Royal Military Academy, Sandhurst.

The journey to Sandhurst was not straightforward for Churchill. His academic challenges at Harrow meant that he was not an obvious candidate for the prestigious military academy. The entrance examinations for Sandhurst were competitive, requiring a level of academic proficiency that Churchill had struggled to demonstrate. It took him three attempts to pass the entrance exams, a testament to his tenacity and refusal to be deterred by failure. This persistence paid off when he was finally admitted, albeit to the cavalry division, which had lower academic requirements than the infantry but required the purchase of more expensive uniforms and horses, underscoring the financial sacrifices his family made for his career.

Once at Sandhurst, Churchill threw himself into the rigors of military training with characteristic zeal. The curriculum was demanding, covering not only academic studies but also physical training, horsemanship, and tactical exercises. It was here that Churchill's strengths began to shine. His keen interest in military history and strategy enriched his understanding of the coursework, and his natural leadership abilities started to emerge more clearly. Churchill excelled in practical military exercises, where he could apply his strategic thinking and boldness in decision-making.

Churchill's time at Sandhurst was also marked by a broadening of his military horizons. He was exposed to the latest theories of warfare and military technology, which were beginning to transform the nature of conflict at the turn of the century. This exposure would later inform his perspectives on military and defense matters, both in his early career as a soldier and journalist and in his later political life.

One of the notable achievements during his tenure at Sandhurst was his improvement in academic standing. Churchill worked diligently to overcome his previous educational shortcomings, demonstrating a capacity for focused study when motivated by his interests. His efforts paid off, as he graduated 20th in his class out of 130 in December 1894, a respectable position that reflected his hard work and determination.

Churchill's graduation from Sandhurst represented more than just the completion of his military training; it was the beginning of his lifelong engagement with the British Army. It provided him with the foundational experiences that would shape his leadership style: a blend of courage, resilience, and strategic acumen.

CHAPTER 2: MILITARY BEGINNINGS AND ADVENTURES

As Winston Churchill stepped beyond the gates of the Royal Military Academy, Sandhurst, his graduation was not merely a ceremonial passage into the British Army; it was the opening chapter of an extraordinary journey that would take him across continents, through the theatres of war, and into the annals of history. Churchill's entry into the military in 1895, as a young officer in the 4th Queen's Own Hussars, was the culmination of his youthful ambitions and the beginning of his lifelong relationship with the armed forces—a relationship that would shape not only his own destiny but also the course of the 20th century.

Churchill's early days in the British military were marked by a mixture of excitement and the rigorous demands of military life. His commission as a second lieutenant in the cavalry was both a privilege and a challenge. The cavalry was seen as a prestigious branch of the service, embodying the romanticism of military tradition and the valor of direct combat.

These initial days were also a time of adaptation and learning. Churchill, ever the keen observer and student of history, immersed himself in the life and routines of a cavalry officer. He took part in the drills, learned the intricacies of cavalry tactics, and built camaraderie with his fellow officers. This period was crucial in developing the practical skills of leadership and command, understanding the responsibilities towards his men, and grasping the complexities of military operations.

Yet, Churchill's ambition and restless spirit sought more than the routine garrison life offered. He was driven by a desire for action and a thirst to witness and participate in the unfolding events of the world stage. This desire would soon lead him beyond the confines of peacetime Britain to the volatile frontiers of the British Empire and beyond, where his courage, intellect, and oratorical skills would be tested in the crucible of conflict.

Even in these early stages of his military career, Churchill was not content with the status quo. He sought out opportunities for action and adventure, looking for postings that would take him to the heart of the empire's conflicts. His first opportunity came in 1895 when he traveled to Cuba to observe the Spanish fight against Cuban guerrillas as a military observer.

Following his time spent in Cuba, Churchill's early military career took him to the far reaches of the British Empire, where he participated in key conflicts that marked the zenith of imperial power and the complexities of colonial rule. These experiences in British India, the Sudan, and the Boer War not only shaped Churchill's views on empire and warfare but also helped forge his reputation as a courageous soldier and a gifted correspondent.

British India: The Northwest Frontier

Churchill's deployment to British India in 1896 as a young army officer was a pivotal chapter in his early military career, offering him his first taste of active service on the Northwest Frontier, a region known for its turbulent history and tribal unrest. This period not only honed Churchill's military acumen but also provided rich material for his burgeoning career as a writer.

Upon joining the 4th Queen's Own Hussars, Churchill was stationed in Banga-
lore, India, a posting that initially offered little in the way of action or adventure.
Eager for combat and keen to make a name for himself, Churchill sought a trans-
fer to the Malakand Field Force, which was being assembled to quell a rebellion
on the Northwest Frontier, a volatile border region near what is now the border
between Pakistan and Afghanistan.

The Malakand Field Force was formed in response to an uprising led by local
tribesmen against British rule. The tribes were rallying around a charismatic reli-
gious leader, the "Mad Fakir," who called for jihad against the British. The campaign was Churchill's first real experience of combat and offered him a firsthand
look at colonial warfare, the complexities of frontier politics, and the difficulties
of military operations in rugged terrain.

Churchill served as both a participant in and observer of the campaign. His duties
involved reconnaissance, engaging in skirmishes, and participating in the relief of
the Malakand garrison, which had come under siege by the tribesmen. The fierce
fighting and challenging conditions of the frontier warfare tested Churchill's
courage and resilience.

Throughout the campaign, Churchill sent detailed dispatches to The Daily Tele-
graph, showcasing not only his experiences and observations but also his ability
to convey the drama and complexity of the conflict to a distant audience. These
dispatches were well-received and marked the beginning of his career as a war
correspondent.

The Sudan: The Battle of Omdurman

Winston Churchill's involvement in the Battle of Omdurman on September
2, 1898, as part of the British campaign to reconquer the Sudan, is a notable
episode in his early military career. This battle was a decisive confrontation that

marked the climax of the Mahdist War, a conflict between the British-Egyptian administration and the Mahdist forces seeking to establish an Islamic state in Sudan. The British-Egyptian forces were led by General Sir Herbert Kitchener, aiming to defeat the Mahdi's successor, Khalifa Abdullah, and avenge the death of General Charles Gordon at Khartoum in 1885.

Churchill, then a young cavalry officer with the 4th Queen's Own Hussars, had managed to secure a temporary attachment to the 21st Lancers, a British cavalry regiment participating in the campaign. Eager for action and adventure, he arrived in Sudan keen to take part in what was to be a demonstration of modern military technology against the dervishes' more traditional methods of warfare.

The British-Egyptian force, equipped with the latest military technology including Maxim guns (early machine guns) and gunboats, advanced on Omdurman, the Mahdist capital near Khartoum. The battle was to be a showcase of the overwhelming firepower and military discipline of Kitchener's forces against the fervent zeal and numerical superiority of the Mahdist fighters.

On the morning of September 2, the British-Egyptian forces engaged the Mahdist army. The battle began with a long-range bombardment by the British artillery, which inflicted heavy casualties on the Mahdists. As the dervishes advanced, they were mowed down by the Maxim guns, demonstrating the devastating effectiveness of machine gunfire against massed infantry charges.

In the midst of this, the 21st Lancers were tasked with a reconnaissance in force towards the Kerreri Hills, northwest of Omdurman. Unbeknownst to them, thousands of Mahdist warriors were concealed in a khor (a dry river bed) near their path. As the Lancers approached, they were suddenly ambushed by the Mahdists, leading to a desperate melee.

Churchill found himself in the thick of the action, participating in one of the last great cavalry charges of the British Army. Armed with a Mauser pistol, he charged into the enemy alongside his fellow soldiers. The Lancers faced fierce resistance, and the engagement was bloody and chaotic. Despite the intensity of the fight, Churchill emerged unscathed, his participation in the charge earning him commendations for bravery.

The Battle of Omdurman was a decisive victory for the British-Egyptian forces. It effectively crushed the Mahdist state and opened the way for the establishment of Anglo-Egyptian rule over Sudan. The battle also served as a grim demonstration of the killing power of modern weaponry, with the Mahdist forces suffering enormous casualties.

Churchill's experiences at Omdurman were profound, and he later recounted them in his book "The River War." He offered not only a detailed account of the campaign but also reflected on the broader implications of the conflict, including the ethics of imperialism and the future of warfare.

The Boer War: Prisoner and Escapee

The outbreak of the Second Boer War in 1899 provided Churchill with another opportunity to combine his military ambitions with his journalistic pursuits. He went to South Africa as a war correspondent for the Morning Post. However, his dual role as a soldier-correspondent saw him actively participating in the conflict.

Churchill was captured by the Boers in November 1899, following the derailment and attack on the armored train he was aboard near Ladysmith, Natal. Despite his civilian status as a correspondent, Churchill's active defense during the attack and his leadership in attempting to free the derailed train under fire convinced the Boers that he was an enemy officer. Consequently, he was transported to a prisoner-of-war camp in Pretoria.

The POW camp was not designed for high security, and the Boers, confident in their ability to monitor the prisoners, did not anticipate escape attempts.

Churchill, however, immediately began planning his escape. He was held in the State Model Schools building, which had been converted into a prison. Conditions were not harsh by the standards of the time, but the young Churchill was determined not to remain a captive.

Churchill's escape occurred on the night of December 12, 1899. The plan was initially conceived with two other prisoners, but when the moment came, only Churchill seized the opportunity to make a dash for freedom. Climbing over a wall while the guards' backs were turned, he found himself alone in enemy territory without a clear plan for reaching British lines.

After escaping, Churchill had to travel approximately 300 miles to Portuguese East Africa (modern-day Mozambique), a neutral territory. The first part of his journey involved hiding in a goods train and then moving on foot, evading capture by relying on his wits and the cover of darkness. His situation was precarious; he had little food, and the region was swarming with Boer patrols on the lookout for the escaped prisoner.

In a stroke of luck, Churchill stumbled upon the house of John Howard, a British mine manager who was sympathetic to the British cause. Howard hid Churchill in a coal mine for several days, during which plans were made for his safe passage to Delagoa Bay in Portuguese East Africa.

With the help of Howard and other British sympathizers, Churchill boarded a freight train and, after a tense journey, finally reached the safety of Portuguese territory. His arrival in Delagoa Bay was met with astonishment and relief. News of his escape quickly spread, turning Churchill into a celebrity and a hero in Britain.

Churchill's daring escape was more than just a personal adventure; it was a propaganda victory for the British, boosting morale at home. Upon his return to Britain, Churchill capitalized on his newfound fame, launching a speaking tour and further establishing himself as a public figure.

CHAPTER 3: ENTRY INTO POLITICS

Upon his return to Britain at the close of his military campaigns, Churchill was already a public figure, celebrated for his daring escape from the Boers and his insightful reporting from the front lines of the British Empire. His books on the campaigns in Sudan and the Northwest Frontier had been well-received, establishing him as a thoughtful commentator on military and imperial affairs. This public profile provided a platform for Churchill's entry into the political arena, where he sought to leverage his experiences and vision for the future of Britain and its empire.

Churchill's decision to enter politics was driven by a belief in his destiny to lead and a desire to play a central role in shaping British policy. He was motivated by the issues of his time, including the need for social reform, the challenges facing the British Empire, and the strategic considerations of an increasingly complex international landscape. His ambition was to be at the heart of decision-making, where he could apply his energy, intellect, and vision to the service of his country.

Churchill's first foray into electoral politics came in 1899 when he contested the Oldham constituency as a Conservative candidate. Despite a spirited campaign, he was unsuccessful, partly due to his absence in South Africa during the Second Boer War. However, his defeat did not deter him. Following his return and the publication of his Boer War despatches, he again contested Oldham in the 1900 general election, this time securing a seat in Parliament.

Churchill's early years in Parliament were marked by his independent streak and willingness to challenge party orthodoxy, particularly on issues of social reform and free trade. His views increasingly aligned him with the Liberal Party, leading to his dramatic decision to "cross the floor" in 1904, abandoning the Conservative Party for the Liberals. This move was controversial, earning him the distrust of many in his former party but also marking him as a politician of principle and conviction.

His tenure in the Liberal Party marked a period of rapid political ascent and significant policy influence, reflecting his adaptability, intellectual versatility, and indefatigable commitment to public service. During his time as a member of the Liberal Party, Churchill served in a number of different roles.

Under-Secretary of State for the Colonies (1905-1908)

Churchill's first major appointment within the Liberal government came in 1905 when he was appointed Under-Secretary of State for the Colonies under Secretary of State Lord Elgin. In this role, Churchill dealt with matters pertaining to the British Empire's vast colonial holdings. He played a part in managing the aftermath of the Second Boer War, advocating for reconciliation and reconstruction in South Africa. His tenure was marked by a progressive stance on colonial governance, emphasizing fairness and the welfare of colonial subjects.

President of the Board of Trade (1908-1910)

In 1908, Churchill was promoted to President of the Board of Trade, becoming the youngest Cabinet minister in over forty years. This role put him at the forefront of domestic economic policy and labor relations. One of his significant achievements was the passage of the Trade Boards Act 1909, which established trade boards to set minimum wages in certain industries, a pioneering move towards modern labor standards. Churchill also played a key role in the development of labor exchanges, which helped workers find employment more efficiently.

Home Secretary (1910-1911)

As Home Secretary, Churchill's responsibilities shifted to internal affairs, including law and order, penal reform, and immigration. His tenure was controversial, marked by his handling of the Tonypandy Riots, where his decision to send troops to support police in quelling coal mining strikes in Wales was widely debated. Another notable incident was the Siege of Sidney Street in 1911, where Churchill's direct involvement in the police operation against armed anarchists in London drew both criticism and admiration.

First Lord of the Admiralty (1911-1915)

When World War I broke out in 1914, Churchill was serving as First Lord of the Admiralty, a position he had held since 1911. He had overseen significant expansions and modernizations of the Royal Navy, preparing it for a major conflict. As the war progressed, the deadlock on the Western Front led the Allied powers to seek alternative strategies to break the stalemate and achieve a decisive victory.

The Ottoman Empire's entry into the war on the side of the Central Powers in October 1914 opened a new front and presented the Allies with both a challenge and an opportunity. Churchill was among the leading proponents of a naval expedition to force the Dardanelles, the narrow strait leading to the Sea of Marmara and ultimately to the Ottoman capital, Constantinople (now Istanbul).

The objective was to open a supply route to Russia and potentially force Turkey out of the war, altering the balance of power in the Allies' favor.

The campaign began in February 1915 with a naval bombardment of Ottoman fortifications along the Dardanelles. However, the naval attack failed to breach the defenses, suffering heavy losses from mines and shore batteries. Despite this setback, Churchill and other advocates of the campaign pushed for an amphibious assault on the Gallipoli Peninsula to capture the strait from the land.

In April 1915, British, Australian, New Zealand, and French troops landed on Gallipoli. They faced fierce resistance from the Ottoman forces, led by commanders such as Mustafa Kemal (later Atatürk). The terrain, underestimated by the Allies, proved to be as much an obstacle as the determined defenders. The campaign quickly bogged down into trench warfare, with both sides suffering heavy casualties.

The Gallipoli campaign dragged on for eight months with little progress and mounting losses. By the end of 1915, it was clear that the venture had failed, and the decision was made to evacuate the Allied forces. The campaign resulted in over 250,000 Allied casualties and a similar number on the Ottoman side.

Churchill's role in the Gallipoli campaign became a subject of intense criticism and controversy. As the architect of the strategy, he bore much of the blame for its failure. The debacle damaged his reputation and led to his demotion within the government. In May 1915, he was removed from his position as First Lord of the Admiralty and later resigned from the government, temporarily sidelining his political career.

Minister of Munitions (1917-1919)

After his resignation from the government in 1915 due to the Gallipoli debacle, Churchill found himself politically isolated. Seeking a return to active service, he spent several months on the Western Front in command of a battalion of the Royal Scots Fusiliers. This period of military service was both a personal proving ground and a political hiatus, but Churchill's ambition and drive for public service remained undiminished.

In July 1917, amidst the backdrop of a world war straining under the immense demands for arms and munitions, Churchill was appointed Minister of Munitions in Prime Minister David Lloyd George's wartime coalition government. His return to the Cabinet was facilitated by the pressing need for energetic and effective leadership in the munitions department, a critical sector for the war effort.

As Minister of Munitions, Churchill inherited a daunting task. The ministry was responsible for ensuring the uninterrupted supply of arms, ammunition, and other war materials to British and Allied forces. The challenges were immense, ranging from managing scarce resources, negotiating labor disputes, and overseeing the expansion of production capabilities, to innovating in the design and manufacture of weaponry.

One of the most pressing issues was the shortage of artillery shells on the Western Front, a problem that had become critically apparent during the Battle of the Somme in 1916. Churchill's approach to resolving the munitions crisis was multifaceted. He worked tirelessly to increase production efficiency, streamline procurement processes, and expand the workforce, including the wider incorporation of women into munitions work.

Under Churchill's leadership, the Ministry of Munitions achieved remarkable increases in production. The output of shells, guns, and other essential war materials grew significantly, contributing to the Allied powers' ability to sustain and eventually escalate their military efforts in the final stages of the war.

Churchill also played a key role in addressing labor unrest in munitions factories. He negotiated with trade unions to ensure that strikes and disputes did not hinder production, balancing workers' rights and demands with the national interest. His efforts helped maintain a relatively stable and productive workforce during a period of potential industrial upheaval.

Churchill's tenure as Minister of Munitions was marked not only by increased production but also by technological innovation. He supported the development of new weapons and tactics, including tanks and chemical warfare, recognizing their potential to break the stalemate on the Western Front.

His work as Minister of Munitions laid the groundwork for the final Allied offensives that would end the war. Moreover, Churchill's successful management of the ministry restored his reputation, proving his worth as a dynamic and capable leader in times of crisis. This period was crucial in rebuilding his political career, setting the stage for his future roles in government and ultimately his leadership during World War II.

Secretary of State for War and Air (1919-1921)

Following World War I, Churchill served as Secretary of State for War and Air, overseeing the demobilization of the British Army and the establishment of the Royal Air Force as an independent service. He was involved in the intervention in the Russian Civil War, supporting the White Russian forces against the Bolsheviks, a policy that reflected his staunch anti-communism.

Secretary of State for the Colonies (1921-1922)

In his final role in the Liberal government, Churchill returned to colonial affairs as Secretary of State for the Colonies. He was instrumental in establishing the British Mandate in Palestine and was involved in the negotiations that led to the creation of the Irish Free State, marking the end of the Irish War of Independence.

Churchill's time with the Liberal Party was characterized by his rapid rise through various high-profile positions, reflecting his broad range of interests and capabilities. His tenure in each role left a lasting impact on British domestic and foreign policy, showcasing his vision, reformist zeal, and leadership qualities that would come to define his storied political career.

CHAPTER 4: THE WILDERNESS YEARS

The year 1922 was a pivotal one for Winston Churchill, marking the beginning of a period often referred to as his "wilderness years," which saw him out of office and politically isolated for much of the next decade. This phase followed his tenure as Secretary of State for the Colonies, a role he held until 1922. His departure from the Liberal Party and the ensuing political isolation were the result of a combination of factors, including shifting political landscapes, personal health issues, and strategic miscalculations.

The Chanak Crisis

One of the immediate catalysts for Churchill's political downturn was the Chanak Crisis in 1922. The crisis centered around the strategic Dardanelles straits, particularly the neutral zone of the Chanak (now Çanakkale), which was under British control following the defeat of the Ottoman Empire in World War I. The Treaty of Sèvres, which had not been ratified by all parties, aimed to dismantle much of the Ottoman Empire and left the straits demilitarized under the control of an international commission. However, the rise of the Turkish Nationalists, led by Mustafa Kemal (later Atatürk), challenged the post-war settlement and sought to renegotiate the terms, leading to the Turkish War of Independence.

In late summer of 1922, Turkish Nationalist forces advanced towards the Dardanelles, threatening the British garrison stationed at Chanak. The prospect of a Kemalist attack posed a significant challenge to the British Empire's control of the straits, a vital link to the Mediterranean and the Black Sea, and thus crucial for both strategic and economic reasons.

As Secretary of State for the Colonies, Churchill was involved in the high-level discussions and decision-making regarding Britain's response to the Turkish advance. Although not directly responsible for military decisions, his hawkish stance and public statements contributed to the atmosphere of tension and the potential for conflict. Churchill was among those in the British government who advocated for a firm response to the Turkish threats, emphasizing the importance of maintaining control over the straits and protecting the interests of the British Empire.

Churchill's position was influenced by his broader views on the British Empire and its role in global affairs. He saw the defense of the straits as not only a matter of strategic necessity but also as a test of Britain's resolve and its commitment to upholding the post-war order established at the Paris Peace Conference.

The crisis was eventually defused through diplomatic negotiations, leading to the signing of the Armistice of Mudanya in October 1922, which ended hostilities and paved the way for the negotiation of the Treaty of Lausanne in 1923. This treaty effectively recognized the sovereignty of the Republic of Turkey and revised the harsh terms imposed by the Treaty of Sèvres.

The Chanak Crisis was a turning point in British foreign policy, demonstrating the limits of post-war British power and the growing reluctance of the British public and its dominions to support unilateral military action. Churchill's aggressive stance during the crisis was seen by some as anachronistic, reflecting a bygone era of imperial dominance. His involvement in the Chanak affair and the broader context of his tenure as Secretary of State for the Colonies contributed to his political isolation in the years that followed.

The Collapse of the Liberal Party

Churchill's political fortunes were also closely tied to the declining fortunes of the Liberal Party. The post-war years saw the British political landscape realigning, with the Labour Party emerging as a significant force and the Conservatives consolidating their position. The Liberal Party, split between the factions led by David Lloyd George and Herbert Asquith, was in decline. Churchill, closely associated with Lloyd George's coalition government, found his political base eroding as the party weakened.

Personal and Health Issues

In 1922, Churchill underwent an operation to remove his appendix, which side-lined him during critical political developments. His convalescence meant he was physically absent from the political scene at a time when his active engagement might have helped navigate the challenges he faced. This personal health issue came at a particularly inopportune moment, exacerbating his political isolation.

The 1922 General Election

The years following World War I were tumultuous for British politics. The Liberal Party, which had dominated British politics in the early 20th century, was deeply fractured between supporters of former Prime Minister David Lloyd George and those of his predecessor, H.H. Asquith. The Conservative Party, meanwhile, was gaining strength, and the Labour Party was emerging as a significant force, capitalizing on the post-war desire for change and reform.

Winston Churchill, who had served as the Secretary of State for the Colonies in Lloyd George's coalition government, was associated with the more interventionist and imperialist policies of the war and post-war period. His stance on various issues, including his opposition to increased home rule for India and his involvement in the Chanak Crisis, had made him a controversial figure.

Churchill had represented Dundee since 1908, initially as a Liberal but later as a coalition Liberal in support of Lloyd George's wartime and post-war governments. Dundee was a two-member constituency, and Churchill had previously been elected alongside a Labour or Asquithian Liberal candidate due to a local electoral pact.

The 1922 general election, held on November 15, came in the wake of the Carlton Club meeting, where the Conservative Party decided to withdraw from the coalition with Lloyd George, effectively ending the post-war coalition government. This decision prompted the general election and placed Churchill, still recovering from an appendectomy, in a difficult position.

Churchill's campaign in Dundee was hampered by several factors. His health was a significant concern; he was still convalescing from his surgery and was unable to campaign with his usual vigor. Additionally, the political climate had shifted, with voters increasingly disillusioned with the coalition government's policies and seeking new leadership.

The Labour Party and the Asquithian Liberals capitalized on the desire for change, making the election a challenging environment for Churchill, who was seen by many as a symbol of the old order. His support for contentious issues, such as the maintenance of British troops in Turkey and opposition to socialism, further alienated him from the electorate.

When the votes were counted, Churchill was defeated, losing his seat to Edwin Scrymgeour, a Prohibitionist representing the Scottish Prohibition Party, and E.D. Morel, an anti-war campaigner from the Labour Party. The loss was a significant personal and political blow to Churchill, leaving him without a parliamentary seat for the first time since entering politics.

Rejoining the Conservative Party

Following his defeat in the 1922 general election and his subsequent loss of the Dundee seat, Churchill found himself politically adrift. The Liberal Party, with which he had been associated since his defection from the Conservatives in 1904, was in decline, fractured between the factions led by H.H. Asquith and David Lloyd George. Meanwhile, the Conservative Party was consolidating its position as the dominant force in British politics, and the Labour Party was emerging as a significant political entity, reflecting the changing social and economic landscape of the country.

During the early 1920s, Churchill's political views increasingly aligned with those of the Conservative Party, especially regarding issues such as opposition to socialism, support for imperial unity, and skepticism towards the Soviet Union. His stance on these and other matters placed him at odds with many in the Liberal Party, which was moving towards a more progressive and social democratic orientation under Asquith's leadership.

The opportunity for Churchill to formalize his return to the Conservative fold came with the general election of October 1924. Earlier that year, Churchill had contested the Westminster Abbey by-election as an independent anti-socialist candidate, signaling his break from the Liberals. Although he was unsuccessful, his campaign drew support from Conservative voters, laying the groundwork for his reintegration into the party.

Stanley Baldwin, the Conservative leader, recognized Churchill's value as a powerful orator and a seasoned politician with a significant public profile. In the run-up to the 1924 election, Baldwin offered Churchill the chance to stand as a Conservative candidate for the Epping constituency, an offer Churchill accepted.

Churchill's decision to stand as a Conservative candidate was tantamount to his formal rejoining of the party he had left two decades earlier. His acceptance of Baldwin's offer reflected both a pragmatic assessment of his political future and a realignment with his original political roots. Churchill's return to the Conservative Party was not without controversy; some party members were wary of his previous defections and his reputation for political opportunism. However, his formidable skills as a statesman and communicator, as well as his alignment with the party's platform on key issues, facilitated his reintegration.

In the general election of 1924, Churchill was elected as the Member of Parliament for Epping, marking his successful return to the House of Commons and the Conservative Party. His victory solidified his political comeback and provided him with a platform to influence British politics for the next several decades.

Personal and Professional Endeavors

The wilderness years were also a time of significant personal and professional development for Churchill. He focused on his writing, producing a number of works that would enhance his reputation as an author and historian. Notably, he penned "The World Crisis," a six-volume history of World War I, and began work on "A History of the English-Speaking Peoples," though its publication would be delayed until after World War II.

Churchill also engaged in painting, a hobby that provided him with great personal solace and a creative outlet during these years. His home at Chartwell became a retreat where he could indulge in his interests away from the political fray.

CHAPTER 5: WORLD WAR II

The "wilderness years" for Winston Churchill came to an end in September 1939, with the outbreak of World War II following the invasion of Poland by Nazi Germany. The global crisis and the imminent threat to Britain and its allies necessitated experienced leadership and a strategic military mindset, qualities that Churchill had in abundance. His persistent warnings about the dangers of Nazi Germany and his advocacy for rearmament and preparedness during the 1930s, once out of sync with the prevailing mood of appeasement, suddenly became highly relevant.

Churchill's Ascent to the Premiership

Churchill's return to prominence coincided with a period of intense crisis for Britain. The rapid advance of German forces across Europe in the spring of 1940, culminating in the Dunkirk evacuation, led to widespread dissatisfaction with Prime Minister Neville Chamberlain's leadership. On May 10, 1940, the same day that Germany launched its invasion of France, Churchill succeeded Chamberlain as Prime Minister. His appointment was the result of a complex political consensus that recognized the need for a leader with Churchill's determination and resolve.

Leadership During the War

Winston Churchill's leadership during World War II is characterized by his remarkable speeches, strategic decisions, and personal involvement in the war effort. His tenure as Prime Minister from 1940 to 1945 saw Britain through some of its darkest days and led to pivotal moments that shaped the outcome of the war.

Churchill's speeches played a critical role in boosting British morale during the war's early and most uncertain days. His words provided the British people with hope, determination, and a sense of unity in the face of adversity. His most famous speeches during this time include:

"Blood, Toil, Tears, and Sweat" (May 13, 1940): Churchill's first speech as Prime Minister to the House of Commons set the tone for his leadership, pledging a relentless fight against Nazi tyranny with resolve and endurance.

"We Shall Fight on the Beaches" (June 4, 1940): After the evacuation of British and Allied troops from Dunkirk, Churchill delivered this speech, vowing to fight the Axis powers across different terrains, never surrendering. This speech is celebrated for its defiance and resolve.

"Their Finest Hour" (June 18, 1940): As Britain braced for a possible invasion, Churchill proclaimed that if the British Empire and its Commonwealth lasted for a thousand years, this would be their finest hour. The speech rallied the nation to stand firm and prepared for the forthcoming Battle of Britain.

The Blitz

"The Blitz" refers to the sustained bombing campaign carried out by Nazi Germany against the United Kingdom during World War II, specifically between September 7, 1940, and May 11, 1941. The term itself is derived from the German word "Blitzkrieg," meaning "lightning war," and it was characterized by frequent and relentless aerial bombings of British cities. London was the primary target, but other major cities such as Coventry, Liverpool, Manchester, and Birmingham also suffered significant damage. The campaign aimed to demoralize the British population, disrupt industrial production, and destroy the country's infrastructure, paving the way for a potential German invasion.

The Blitz began after the failure of the German Luftwaffe to gain air superiority over the Royal Air Force (RAF) during the Battle of Britain in the summer of 1940. Unable to secure a decisive victory, Adolf Hitler and Reichsmarschall Hermann Göring shifted their strategy towards large-scale bombing raids on British cities. The bombings were initially concentrated on London, with attacks occurring for 56 out of the 57 consecutive nights following the campaign's commencement. Over the course of the Blitz, around 43,000 civilians were killed, and more than a million homes destroyed or damaged in London alone.

Throughout the Blitz, Winston Churchill's leadership became a beacon of resilience and defiance against the Nazi aggression. His actions and decisions during this period were pivotal in maintaining British morale and resistance. During this testing time, Churchill's actions included:

Visits to Bombed Areas: Churchill frequently visited areas devastated by the bombings, often immediately following an air raid. These visits were not mere symbolic gestures; they provided a crucial morale boost to the British public. Photographs and newsreels of Churchill walking among the ruins, talking to civilians and emergency services personnel, became iconic. These images underscored his solidarity with the suffering of ordinary people and bolstered his reputation as a leader who shared in the nation's hardships.

Speeches and Broadcasts: Churchill's speeches during the Blitz were instrumental in rallying the British people. His words offered comfort, courage, and a resolve to persevere and ultimately triumph over the Axis powers. Through radio broadcasts, he reached millions of listeners, not just in Britain but around the world, articulating a vision of steadfastness and victory.

Strategic Leadership: Beyond his inspirational role, Churchill was deeply involved in the strategic response to the Blitz. He worked closely with military and civil defense leaders to coordinate the nation's defenses and ensure the continuity of government operations. Under his leadership, measures such as the expansion of anti-aircraft defenses, the development of the Home Guard, and the enhancement of fire-fighting and air raid precautions were intensified.

Advocating for Allied Support: Recognizing the need for a stronger Allied response to Nazi aggression, Churchill used the Blitz to galvanize support from the United States and other allies. His communication with President Franklin D. Roosevelt during this time helped to secure vital aid through the Lend-Lease Act, which was instrumental in bolstering Britain's ability to withstand and eventually counter the Axis powers.

The Blitz remains one of the most harrowing periods of British history, yet it also stands as a testament to the resilience and courage of the British people. Churchill's leadership during this time—marked by his personal courage, strategic foresight, and ability to communicate hope amidst despair—played an indispensable role in sustaining the nation's morale. The Blitz forged a sense of unity and determination that would carry Britain through the darkest days of the war and contribute significantly to the eventual Allied victory.

Strategic Decisions and Military Leadership

Churchill was involved in strategic decisions that had far-reaching implications for the course of the war:

The Battle of Britain (July-October 1940): Churchill's support for the Royal Air Force (RAF) and recognition of its significance in preventing a German invasion was crucial. His tribute to the RAF, "Never in the field of human conflict was so much owed by so many to so few," underscored the importance of air power in the conflict.

The North African Campaign: Churchill was instrumental in the decision to prioritize the North African campaign, leading to the victory at El Alamein under General Bernard Montgomery in October 1942. This victory was a turning point, as Churchill noted, "Before Alamein we never had a victory. After Alamein, we never had a defeat."

The D-Day Invasion (June 6, 1944): Churchill played a key role in planning and supporting the Allied invasion of Normandy, which was a critical step towards liberating Europe from Nazi occupation.

Relationship with Allied Leaders

Winston Churchill's relationships with Allied leaders during World War II were crucial to the formulation and success of the Allied strategy against the Axis powers. These relationships, particularly with U.S. President Franklin D. Roosevelt and Soviet Premier Joseph Stalin, were complex, marked by a blend of mutual respect, strategic necessity, and, at times, profound disagreement. Churchill's diplomatic skill and personal charisma played significant roles in navigating these alliances.

Relationship with Franklin D. Roosevelt

Churchill's relationship with Franklin D. Roosevelt was foundational to the British-American alliance, which became the cornerstone of the Allied effort during the war. This partnership was built on shared values and strategic interests, though it was not without its challenges.

The relationship began through correspondence even before the United States entered the war in December 1941. Churchill's first letter to Roosevelt, sent in September 1939, sought American support, marking the beginning of a prolific exchange that would continue throughout the war.

A pivotal moment in their relationship came with the U.S. Lend-Lease Act of March 1941, which allowed the U.S. to supply the UK and other Allied nations with military materiel. This act, significantly supported by Roosevelt, was crucial in providing Britain with the resources needed to continue fighting.

Churchill and Roosevelt met several times during the war, beginning with the Atlantic Conference in August 1941. This meeting resulted in the Atlantic Charter, outlining the Allies' post-war vision. Subsequent meetings at conferences such as Casablanca, Tehran, and Yalta were instrumental in defining Allied strategy.

While there was a genuine respect and friendship between the two leaders, their relationship was not devoid of tension. Differences over strategy, particularly concerning the timing of the D-Day invasion and the post-war reconstruction, occasionally strained their partnership.

Relationship with Joseph Stalin

Churchill's relationship with Joseph Stalin was more pragmatic and often fraught with suspicion and ideological differences. Despite this, the necessity of defeating Nazi Germany led to a crucial, if uneasy, alliance.

Churchill was initially wary of the Soviet Union and its intentions in Eastern Europe. However, the German invasion of the Soviet Union in June 1941 forced a realignment of strategies, bringing the USSR into the Allied fold.

Churchill met Stalin in person for the first time at the Tehran Conference in 1943, along with Roosevelt. This meeting was crucial in securing Soviet support for the planned invasion of Western Europe (D-Day) and in discussing post-war arrangements for Europe. The Yalta Conference in February 1945 further addressed the reorganization of post-war Europe, although decisions made there would later contribute to the onset of the Cold War.

Churchill's approach to Stalin was characterized by realpolitik; he recognized the necessity of Soviet participation in the war effort despite misgivings about communist ideology and Stalin's post-war ambitions. Their relationship was marked by a mix of diplomatic flattery, frank discussions, and hard bargaining.

Challenges and Controversies

Churchill's tenure as British Prime Minister during World War II, while marked by his iconic leadership and oratory, also faced significant challenges and controversies. Two of the most notable and debated aspects of his wartime leadership were the strategic bombing of German cities and his government's handling of the Bengal Famine of 1943.

Strategic Bombing of German Cities

The strategic bombing campaign against Germany, conducted by the Royal Air Force (RAF) and later by both the RAF and the United States Army Air Forces (USAAF), was aimed at crippling German industrial capacity, undermining civilian morale, and supporting military operations by destroying infrastructure. As the war progressed, the campaign escalated in intensity, leading to widespread destruction and significant civilian casualties in German cities.

Churchill's involvement and support for the bombing campaign were rooted in the strategic imperative to weaken Nazi Germany's ability to wage war. However, the campaign, particularly the bombing of cities like Dresden in February 1945, which resulted in the deaths of an estimated 25,000 people, has been a subject of historical debate and moral scrutiny. Critics argue that the bombings were disproportionate and targeted civilian areas, straying from purely military objectives and violating principles of warfare. Churchill himself expressed concerns about the "area bombing" strategy's moral implications in a memo sent to his air chiefs, questioning the extent and necessity of targeting German cities with such ferocity, especially as the war neared its end.

The Bengal Famine of 1943

The Bengal Famine of 1943 was one of the most devastating humanitarian disasters of the 20th century, resulting in the deaths of an estimated 2 to 3 million people in British-ruled India. The famine was caused by a combination of factors, including wartime disruption, crop failure, and policy failures. Churchill's government has been criticized for its inadequate response to the crisis and for prioritizing military needs over humanitarian considerations.

Critics argue that the British war effort's demands exacerbated the famine by diverting resources away from India, including shipping that could have been used to import food. Additionally, the British government's policy of stockpiling food and implementing a scorched earth policy in response to Japanese threats further strained food availability in Bengal. Churchill's personal attitude towards India and its people has also been scrutinized, with some attributing a lack of urgency in his response to the famine to his imperialist views.

While defenders of Churchill argue that the wartime context and the global nature of the war effort limited the capacity of the British government to respond more effectively to the famine, the tragedy remains a significant blot on Churchill's legacy.

The 1945 General Election

The 1945 general election in the United Kingdom, held on July 5th but not declared until July 26th to allow votes from servicemen overseas to be counted, was a landmark event in British political history. Despite Winston Churchill's immense popularity as a wartime leader, his Conservative Party suffered a landslide defeat to Clement Attlee's Labour Party. This election is notable for several reasons, including its timing immediately after World War II, the public's appetite for social change, and the contrasting visions for post-war Britain presented by the two leading parties.

As World War II drew to a close in Europe, there was a growing consensus within Britain that significant social, economic, and political reforms were necessary to address the inequalities and hardships that had been exacerbated by the war. The Labour Party, having been a junior partner in the wartime coalition government, campaigned on a platform of comprehensive social reform, including the creation of a welfare state, nationalization of key industries, and the implementation of the Beveridge Report's recommendations, which outlined a plan for social security that would free people from the "five giants" of want, disease, ignorance, squalor, and idleness.

Churchill's campaign strategy, in contrast, emphasized the dangers of socialism and Labour's proposed economic policies, which he argued would stifle freedom and individual initiative. In a widely criticized speech, Churchill even suggested that a Labour government would require some form of a "Gestapo" to implement its policies, implying that Labour's socialist agenda could lead to totalitarianism. This comparison not only failed to resonate with the electorate, many of whom were soldiers returning from fighting against fascism, but also backfired, painting Churchill as out of touch with the domestic issues facing post-war Britain.

The results of the election were shocking to many, including Labour leaders themselves. Labour won 393 seats, giving them a hefty majority in the House of Commons, while the Conservatives secured only 197 seats. This landslide victory for Labour was seen as a mandate for change, with the British public demonstrating a clear desire for comprehensive social and economic reform to rebuild Britain after the war.

CHAPTER 6: POSTWAR YEARS

Following the Labour Party's landslide victory in July 1945, Churchill found himself ousted from Downing Street, replaced by Clement Attlee. Despite the initial shock, Churchill did not retreat from public life. Instead, he assumed the role of Leader of the Opposition, critiquing the Labour government's policies with the same vigor he had applied to fighting the Axis powers.

Churchill's "Iron Curtain" Speech

Winston Churchill's "Iron Curtain" speech, officially titled "The Sinews of Peace," delivered on March 5, 1946, at Westminster College in Fulton, Missouri, is considered one of the most significant orations of the 20th century. It marked the beginning of the Cold War public discourse, articulating the division of Europe into two opposing ideological blocs and underscoring the emerging geopolitical tension between the Western Allies and the Soviet Union.

Following the end of World War II, Europe was devastated, and the process of rebuilding was underway. The United States and the Soviet Union emerged as the two superpowers, but their wartime alliance quickly deteriorated due to ideological differences and conflicting interests in the post-war world. While the Western Allies advocated for democracy and free enterprise, the Soviet Union aimed to expand its influence and establish communist governments in Eastern Europe.

In his speech, Churchill vividly described the division of Europe by an "iron curtain" that had descended from the Baltic to the Adriatic Sea, separating the Soviet-controlled east from the democracies of the west. He highlighted the Soviet Union's expansion and the imposition of communist regimes in Eastern European countries, emphasizing the threat this posed to freedom and security.

Churchill called for a strong partnership between the United States and Britain, along with other like-minded nations, to counter the Soviet threat. He advocated for the "fraternal association" of the English-speaking world, emphasizing the importance of the United Nations but also suggesting the need for a regional approach to security, foreshadowing the formation of NATO in 1949.

The speech was not a call to arms but rather a call for vigilance and unity among the Western democracies to protect freedom and promote peace. Churchill's use of the term "iron curtain" captured the imagination of the public and became a defining metaphor for the Cold War.

The reaction to Churchill's speech was mixed. In the United States, it received considerable support, especially among those who were concerned about Soviet actions in Europe. President Harry S. Truman, who had introduced Churchill at Westminster College, was aware of the speech's content in advance and saw it as a reflection of the changing American attitude towards the Soviet Union.

In contrast, the speech was met with hostility by the Soviet Union. Soviet leader Joseph Stalin denounced it as warmongering and an attack on the Soviet Union. Critics on the left in Britain and the United States also accused Churchill of exacerbating tensions with the Soviet Union.

The Founding of the United Nations

One of Churchill's significant contributions to the principles that would later underpin the United Nations was the Atlantic Charter. In August 1941, Churchill and Roosevelt met aboard the HMS Prince of Wales off the coast of Newfoundland. Although the United States had not yet entered World War II, both leaders were concerned about the post-war world order. The Atlantic Charter was a pivotal declaration that outlined their vision for a world free from tyranny, marked by disarmament, self-determination, economic cooperation, and social welfare. These principles later influenced the UN Charter's formulation, emphasizing peace, security, and international cooperation.

The formal establishment of the United Nations occurred through the United Nations Conference on International Organization, held in San Francisco from April 25 to June 26, 1945. Representatives from 50 nations gathered to draft the UN Charter, which was signed on June 26, 1945. The charter established the UN's structure, including the Security Council, General Assembly, International Court of Justice, and various other bodies aimed at promoting peace, security, and cooperation.

While Churchill did not participate directly in the San Francisco Conference, his wartime leadership, advocacy for international cooperation against the Axis powers, and the promotion of post-war reconstruction and peace laid part of the philosophical and political groundwork for the UN's creation. Churchill's vision of a "United Nations," a term he and Roosevelt used to describe the Allies against the Axis powers, contributed to the naming and spirit of the organization.

Churchill's Writings

One of Churchill's most monumental writing projects during this period was his six-volume history, "The Second World War," published between 1948 and

1953. Although the majority of this work was completed and published after he returned to office in 1951, much of the research and writing took place during these interim years. In this series, Churchill provided a detailed account of the war, blending meticulous historical research with his personal insights and experiences as Prime Minister during the conflict. The work was both a critical and commercial success, offering invaluable perspectives on the war's events and decisions. It reinforced Churchill's status as a key figure in history and provided him with significant financial rewards, helping to alleviate the considerable debts he had accumulated.

Another major writing project that Churchill undertook during this period was "A History of the English-Speaking Peoples." Originally conceived in the 1930s, Churchill resumed work on this project after World War II. The four-volume series, which covered the history of Britain and the United States from the Anglo-Saxon period to the early 20th century, was completed during his second term as Prime Minister but published later, starting in 1956. This work further established Churchill as a prominent historian and reflected his deep belief in the special relationship between Britain and the United States.

The 1950 General Election

The 1950 general election in the United Kingdom, held on February 23, 1950, played a crucial role in setting the stage for Winston Churchill's return to the premiership in 1951. This election was significant for several reasons, marking a transition period in British post-war politics and reflecting the changing dynamics within the electorate and the political landscape. While the Labour Party, led by Clement Attlee, won the election, its reduced majority set the scene for another general election just over a year later, in which Churchill would make his comeback.

The Labour Party had won a landslide victory in the 1945 general election, implementing an ambitious programme of social and economic reforms, including the nationalization of key industries and the creation of the National Health Service. By 1950, however, Britain was still recovering from the war's devastations, grappling with economic challenges such as austerity measures, rationing, and a large national debt.

The 1950 election was the first general election since the end of World War II to be held under more normal peacetime conditions. The Labour Party sought a mandate to continue its programme of reforms, while the Conservative Party, under Churchill's leadership, campaigned for a change in direction, promising to ease austerity measures and to review the nationalization policies.

Labour won the election but with a significantly reduced majority, securing 315 seats out of 625, down from 393 in the 1945 election. This slender majority of just five seats made governing difficult, especially with a parliament that was more evenly divided and with post-war challenges that required strong and decisive action.

The Conservative Party made substantial gains, winning 298 seats, an increase from their previous tally. The election results demonstrated that public support for the Conservatives was growing, partly due to dissatisfaction with ongoing rationing and austerity, as well as concerns about Britain's economic situation.

For Winston Churchill, the 1950 election results were encouraging, even though he did not win. The gains made by the Conservatives under his leadership suggested that there was a significant appetite for change among the British electorate. The results also reinforced Churchill's position as the leader of the Conservative Party and the main challenger to the Labour government.

Health Challenges

Between his first term as Prime Minister during World War II and his second premiership beginning in 1951, Winston Churchill faced several significant health challenges. These issues impacted both his political career and personal life, testing his resilience and influencing perceptions of his capacity to lead, especially given his advancing age.

Perhaps the most serious health challenge Churchill faced during this period was a stroke in 1949, which was kept secret from the public. The stroke occurred while Churchill was on vacation in the South of France. It was severe enough to affect his speech and mobility for a period, raising concerns among his inner circle about his ability to continue in active political life. His remarkable recovery was testament to his determination, but the incident left him with lingering effects that would be managed in secrecy.

Churchill also suffered from ischemic heart disease, experiencing several minor heart attacks during the late 1940s and early 1950s. These incidents, while not publicly disclosed at the time, contributed to concerns about his overall cardiovascular health.

The intense demands of leadership during World War II, followed by the pressures of leading the opposition and his own personal drive to remain active in politics and writing, took a physical toll on Churchill. He often worked late into the night and had a lifestyle that included heavy drinking and cigar smoking, which, despite his robust constitution, contributed to his overall health decline.

The 1951 General Election

The 1951 general election in the United Kingdom, held on October 25th, marked a pivotal moment in British post-war politics and the culmination of Winston Churchill's political comeback. Despite the Conservative Party securing fewer total votes than the Labour Party, Churchill managed to win a majority of seats in the House of Commons, enabling him to return to the office of Prime Minister. This election is notable for several factors, including the context of its occurrence, the strategies employed by the Conservative Party, and the broader public sentiment that influenced its outcome.

The election came after six years of Labour government under Clement Attlee, which had implemented significant social and economic reforms, including the creation of the National Health Service and the nationalization of key industries. However, by 1951, Britain was still grappling with economic difficulties, including continued rationing and austerity measures, which had become increasingly unpopular among the British public. Moreover, the Labour government faced internal divisions and challenges, including health issues affecting key figures like Attlee and Ernest Bevin.

The Conservative Party, led by Winston Churchill, capitalized on public fatigue with austerity and promised to end rationing and improve the economy. They also pledged to maintain the newly established welfare state, easing fears that a Conservative government would dismantle Labour's social reforms. The Conservatives' manifesto emphasized themes of recovery, prosperity, and strength against the backdrop of the ongoing Cold War. Churchill's personal leadership and his status as a war hero played a central role in the campaign, with the Conservatives leveraging his image to garner support.

The Labour Party campaigned on its record of establishing the welfare state and its plans for further social and economic reforms. However, the party was hampered by public perception of economic mismanagement and by internal divisions over future policy directions. Additionally, the wear and tear of governing through difficult post-war years had taken its toll on Labour's leadership, contributing to a sense of a government in need of renewal.

The election results were closely contested. The Conservative Party won 321 seats out of 625 in the House of Commons, securing a slim majority. Labour, despite receiving more total votes due to the distribution of votes and the first-past-the-post electoral system, won 295 seats. This outcome was sufficient for Churchill to form a government and return to Downing Street as Prime Minister.

CHAPTER 7: SECOND PREMIERSHIP

Winston Churchill's second term as Prime Minister, from October 1951 to April 1955, marked a period of both consolidation and challenge. Returning to power at the age of 76, Churchill's leadership style had evolved, focusing more on international affairs and delegating much of the domestic policy to his cabinet colleagues. Despite his advancing age and health issues, Churchill's tenure was marked by several significant policies and challenges.

Domestic Policies and Changes

Housing and Construction: One of the main domestic priorities of Churchill's government was addressing the post-war housing shortage. Under the leadership of Harold Macmillan, who served as Minister of Housing and Local Government, the government embarked on an ambitious program to build 300,000 houses a year, a target that was largely met. This effort helped alleviate the housing crisis and was a significant achievement of Churchill's second administration.

Health and Welfare: While the Conservative government maintained the welfare state established by the Labour Party, it introduced some changes. The government sought to reduce the financial strain on the National Health Service (NHS) by introducing prescription charges and dental and ophthalmic charges.

These measures were controversial, as they represented a departure from the NHS's founding principles of being free at the point of use.

Economic Policies: Churchill's government faced the challenge of managing the British economy in the post-war period, focusing on controlling inflation and maintaining employment levels. The government also navigated the transition from wartime to peacetime economy, overseeing the end of rationing by 1954, which was a significant milestone in the recovery from the war's impact.

International Affairs and Challenges

The Cold War: Churchill's second premiership occurred during the height of the Cold War, and he played a significant role in shaping Western strategy against the Soviet Union. Churchill continued to advocate for a strong NATO alliance and sought to maintain the special relationship with the United States, although his relationship with President Dwight D. Eisenhower was more pragmatic than the close personal friendship he had with Franklin D. Roosevelt.

European Integration: Churchill supported the idea of European unity but was cautious about Britain's involvement in European integration efforts. He famously advocated for a "United States of Europe" in which Britain would be a supporter but not a member, reflecting his vision of Britain's global role as being distinct from Europe.

Nuclear Deterrent: Churchill's government was instrumental in developing Britain's independent nuclear deterrent, recognizing the strategic importance of nuclear weapons in Cold War diplomacy. The decision to proceed with the development of the British hydrogen bomb during his tenure was a significant step in establishing Britain as a nuclear power.

Health and Leadership Challenges

Churchill's Health: Throughout his second term, Churchill's health was a significant concern. He suffered a serious stroke in June 1953, which temporarily incapacitated him and was kept secret from the public and most of the government. His recovery was slow, and there were calls for him to resign, although he eventually returned to his duties.

Succession Issues: Churchill's health issues brought the question of his successor to the forefront. There was considerable uncertainty and internal party jockeying over who would follow him as leader of the Conservative Party and Prime Minister. Eventually, Anthony Eden succeeded Churchill when he resigned in April 1955.

CHAPTER 8: FINAL YEARS

Winston Churchill's final years after stepping down as Prime Minister in April 1955 were marked by a gradual withdrawal from the intense political life that had defined much of his career. Even as his public engagements lessened due to advancing age and declining health, Churchill remained a figure of immense respect and influence, both in Britain and around the world. His last decade was a period of reflection, recognition, and the cementing of his legacy as one of the 20th century's most significant figures.

Continued Public Life

After stepping down as Prime Minister in April 1955, Winston Churchill continued to serve as a Member of Parliament (MP) for Woodford until he retired from the House of Commons at the 1964 general election. This period marked the twilight of his extraordinary political career, spanning nearly six decades.

During these final years as an MP, Churchill's direct contributions to legislative debates and parliamentary proceedings were limited. His declining health and advanced age meant that his attendance at the House of Commons became increasingly infrequent. Nonetheless, Churchill remained a deeply respected figure within the Conservative Party and the broader political landscape, and his rare appearances in the Commons were events of note.

As the 1964 general election approached, Churchill, then in his late 80s, decided not to seek re-election. His decision marked the end of an era in British politics. In his retirement announcement, Churchill expressed gratitude to the electorate of Woodford, whom he had served for over 30 years. His retirement from Parliament was a moment of national reflection on his immense contributions to Britain and the world.

Health Challenges

It's worth noting that Churchill had already experienced significant health issues before his retirement from the premiership, including a severe stroke in June 1953, while he was still in office. This stroke temporarily incapacitated him, affecting his speech and mobility, though he made a partial recovery and returned to his duties.

Churchill suffered several more strokes in the years following his resignation. A particularly severe one in 1956 left him physically weakened and further impaired his ability to speak and walk. These episodes were kept relatively private, with the severity of his condition often downplayed to the public.

Churchill's mobility was increasingly limited, and he was prone to falls. In 1960, he fractured his hip after a fall, which further impacted his physical capabilities and required a lengthy recovery period. His resilience in the face of these physical setbacks was notable, but they undoubtedly took a toll on his overall health.

There were also signs of cognitive decline in his final years, with reports of memory lapses and periods of confusion. This was likely exacerbated by his strokes and the general decline in his physical health.

Recognition and Honors

In the years following his second premiership, Winston Churchill continued to receive significant recognition and honors, reflecting his monumental contributions to Britain and the world.

In 1953, Winston Churchill was knighted by Queen Elizabeth II, receiving the Garter, the highest order of knighthood in the United Kingdom. The honor recognized his service to the nation, particularly his leadership during World War II. Churchill became Sir Winston Churchill, KG (Knight of the Garter), an acknowledgment that placed him among the most esteemed figures in British society. Unlike some other orders of British chivalry, the Order of the Garter is awarded at the sovereign's discretion, without advice from the government, emphasizing the personal esteem in which Churchill was held by the Queen.

Also in 1953, Churchill was awarded the Nobel Prize in Literature "for his mastery of historical and biographical description as well as for brilliant oratory in defending exalted human values." The award was a testament to his dual career as a statesman and an author, recognizing his vast body of written work, including his speeches, histories, and memoirs. Churchill's literary output was not only prolific but also of significant historical value, offering insights into the events of his time and the principles that guided his political career. The Nobel Prize acknowledged the unique contribution of Churchill's writings to the cultural and intellectual heritage of the world.

Churchill was also granted honorary citizenship of the United States in 1963 by President John F. Kennedy, an honor that had been bestowed on only seven other individuals by that time. This recognition highlighted the special relationship between the United Kingdom and the United States, as well as Churchill's personal role in fostering that bond.

Final Public Appearance

Winston Churchill's final significant public appearance was during the unveiling of his portrait by artist Graham Sutherland on November 30, 1954, a ceremony held in Westminster Hall, Parliament, to commemorate Churchill's 80th birthday. The event was notable not just for marking one of the last public honors bestowed upon Churchill but also for the controversy surrounding the portrait itself.

The unveiling was a significant occasion, attended by a distinguished audience including members of both Houses of Parliament. This event was symbolic, intended to honor Churchill's vast contributions to the nation through his decades of public service and, most notably, his leadership during World War II. The portrait was commissioned by members of the House of Commons and the House of Lords as a gesture of the high esteem in which Churchill was held.

Graham Sutherland, a prominent British artist known for his modernist and somewhat abstract style, was tasked with creating the portrait. The artwork was meant to be a realistic and insightful depiction of Churchill at 80, capturing the essence of his character and the weight of his legacy. However, the final piece—a portrayal of Churchill seated, looking somewhat pensive and burdened—was not well-received by Churchill or his family. Churchill humorously remarked on its portrayal of him, indicating his displeasure and famously describing it as "a remarkable example of modern art," with a tone of irony suggesting his dissatisfaction.

Despite the public honor the portrait's commission represented, its reception by Churchill highlighted his complex relationship with his own legacy and public image. The portrait was intended to be a part of the national collection, but it was reportedly taken to Chartwell, Churchill's family home, and was never displayed publicly during his lifetime. Following Churchill's death in 1965, the portrait was mysteriously destroyed, an act later revealed to have been carried out at the behest of his wife, Clementine Churchill, who shared her husband's disapproval of the piece.

Legacy

Winston Churchill passed away on January 24, 1965, at the age of 90. His state funeral, held on January 30, was a moment of national mourning and global tribute, attended by world leaders and watched by millions around the world. Churchill was buried in the family plot at St Martin's Church, Bladon, near his birthplace at Blenheim Palace, in accordance with his wishes.

Churchill's legacy is vast and complex, encompassing his roles as a military leader, statesman, historian, and orator. He is remembered for his indomitable spirit, his leadership during Britain's darkest hours, and his contributions to the Allied victory in World War II. Churchill's speeches and writings continue to inspire, and his life's work remains a subject of study and admiration.

Beyond his achievements, Churchill's legacy includes a profound impact on the values of courage, determination, and perseverance in the face of adversity. His personal motto, "Never give in," encapsulates the spirit with which he approached both his public duties and personal challenges, leaving a lasting imprint on the British national consciousness and the broader course of history.

CHAPTER 9: LIFE OUTSIDE OF POLITICS

Beyond the indomitable public persona and the relentless drive that characterized his political career, Winston Churchill's life outside the political arena was rich with personal interests, family commitments, and hobbies that provided him solace, joy, and a counterbalance to his demanding public life.

Family Life

Winston Churchill married Clementine Hozier in September 1908, and their marriage was a lasting partnership that endured the tumultuous ups and downs of Churchill's career. Clementine was not only a steadfast supporter of her husband but also an influential figure in her own right, often advising Churchill on political and social issues. The Churchills had five children: Diana, Randolph, Sarah, Marigold (who died tragically at the age of two), and Mary. The loss of Marigold was a profound sorrow for both Winston and Clementine.

Churchill was known to be a devoted, if sometimes distant, father. His demanding career often kept him away from home, but he maintained close relationships with his children, especially in his later years. His daughter Mary, in particular, became an important source of support and companionship in Churchill's old age.

Hobbies and Interests

In the rare times that he found himself not working, Winston Churchill engaged in a variety of hobbies, notably including:

Painting: One of Churchill's most famous hobbies was painting, an activity he took up in his 40s. Painting offered him a mental refuge from the stresses of his career, allowing him a form of expression that was entirely his own. Churchill preferred landscapes and still lifes, and he painted with a bright and bold palette. His works were exhibited under the pseudonym "Charles Morin," and he took great pride in his art, finding in it a satisfaction that politics could not always provide.

Bricklaying and Landscaping: At his family home, Chartwell, Churchill indulged in bricklaying and landscaping. He took a hands-on approach to the property's improvements, constructing walls and buildings on the estate. These activities were not mere pastimes; they were pursuits that allowed Churchill to engage physically and creatively in projects entirely separate from his public duties.

Writing: Churchill was a prolific writer, and his literary career was both a professional endeavor and a personal passion. His historical works, memoirs, and speeches not only earned him the Nobel Prize in Literature but also provided an outlet for reflection on his vast experiences and the tumultuous times he lived through. Writing was an integral part of Churchill's identity, bridging his public and private lives.

Travel: Churchill loved to travel, especially to warm climates for holidays. His travels were not only for relaxation but also provided him with new perspectives and inspirations for both his political and personal projects.

Personal Characteristics

Churchill's personal life was marked by contradictions. He could be both gregarious and solitary, deeply sensitive yet often brusque. His capacity for deep friendship was evident in his close relationships with a circle of trusted advisers and colleagues. Yet, he also required periods of isolation, retreating to Chartwell or holiday homes in the South of France to think, write, and paint.

Despite the public perception of Churchill as a stern and formidable figure, those who knew him personally often spoke of his wit, his capacity for kindness, and his sentimental nature. His love for animals, especially his poodles Rufus I and II, highlighted a gentler side to the man known for his bulldog tenacity.

CHAPTER 10: CHURCHILL THE AUTHOR

Winston Churchill was not only one of the 20th century's most influential political figures but also a prolific author whose literary output spanned a variety of genres, including history, biography, and memoir. His works were critically acclaimed and earned him the Nobel Prize in Literature in 1953 "for his mastery of historical and biographical description as well as for brilliant oratory in defending exalted human values." This chapter delves into Churchill's major literary works, exploring their themes, reception, and the unique insights they offer into the author's mind.

"The Story of the Malakand Field Force" (1898)

One of Churchill's earliest works, this book is an account of his experiences as a young army officer and war correspondent during the Malakand expedition in the North-West Frontier Province (now in Pakistan). The book blends military history with personal observations, showcasing Churchill's burgeoning literary talent and keen insight into military affairs. It was well-received, highlighting his potential as both a soldier and a writer.

"The River War" (1899)

An account of the British-Egyptian reconquest of the Sudan (1896-1899), "The River War" is notable for its detailed military analysis and critique of British imperial policy. The work reflects Churchill's first-hand observations as a participant in the campaign and establishes his reputation as a serious historian. Its candid and sometimes critical view of British actions was controversial but demonstrated Churchill's commitment to a nuanced understanding of history.

"My Early Life" (1930)

This engaging autobiography covers Churchill's adventures from childhood up to 1902, including his time as a soldier and journalist in India, Sudan, and South Africa. Known for its wit and vivid storytelling, "My Early Life" offers insight into the formative experiences that shaped Churchill's character and career. It remains one of his most popular works, celebrated for its humanizing portrayal of the future leader.

"The Second World War" (1948-1953)

Perhaps Churchill's most monumental work, this six-volume history offers an exhaustive account of World War II from his unique perspective as Britain's wartime Prime Minister. The series combines comprehensive historical detail with Churchill's personal insights and documents, providing an invaluable record of the conflict. While some critics have noted the work's subjective slant, it is widely regarded as an essential source for understanding World War II and won Churchill international acclaim, including the Nobel Prize in Literature.

"A History of the English-Speaking Peoples" (1956-1958)

Conceived in the 1930s but published after his final retirement from politics, this four-volume series traces the development of English-speaking nations from the earliest times to the early 20th century. While criticized by some historians for its anglophone bias and occasional inaccuracies, the work is praised for its narrative style and Churchill's ability to weave together complex historical threads. It reflects his deep belief in the shared destiny and values of English-speaking peoples.

Reception and Legacy

Churchill's writings were generally well-received by both critics and the public, contributing significantly to his financial stability and global reputation. His historical works, in particular, have been praised for their detailed research, compelling narratives, and the unique perspective Churchill brings as a central figure in many of the events he describes. However, his works have also been critiqued for their imperialist viewpoint and personal biases, reflecting the complex figure Churchill himself was.

Throughout his literary career, Churchill demonstrated a remarkable ability to communicate complex ideas and historical events with clarity, eloquence, and a distinctive voice. His contributions to literature not only enrich our understanding of the events of his time but also offer a window into the mind of one of history's most fascinating characters.

CHAPTER 11: WINSTON CHURCHILL – A TIMELINE

The following timeline details key events in the life of Winston Churchill, a figure whose career spanned some of the most pivotal moments in the 20th century. From his early years to his final days, Churchill's journey was marked by remarkable achievements, challenges, and an enduring legacy.

Early Years and Education

1874: Born on November 30th at Blenheim Palace, Oxfordshire, England.

1888-1892: Attends Harrow School, where he initially struggles but eventually excels in English and History.

1893-1895: Studies at the Royal Military College, Sandhurst, graduating 20th in his class.

Military Career

1895: Joins the 4th Queen's Own Hussars; travels to Cuba as a military observer.

1897: Participates in the Malakand campaign on the Northwest Frontier of British India.

1898: Takes part in the Battle of Omdurman in the Sudan.

1899-1902: Serves as a correspondent and combatant in the Second Boer War in South Africa, where he is captured and makes a dramatic escape.

Early Political Career

1900: Elected to Parliament as a Conservative MP for Oldham.

1904: Defects to the Liberal Party over policy differences.

1908: Marries Clementine Hozier on September 12th; they have five children over their marriage.

1911: Appointed First Lord of the Admiralty, overseeing the Royal Navy in the lead-up to WWI.

World War I and Interwar Period

1915: Assumes responsibility for the failed Gallipoli campaign, leading to his resignation from the Admiralty.

1917: Appointed Minister of Munitions, contributing to the WWI effort on the home front.

1924: Returns to the Conservative Party; appointed Chancellor of the Exchequer.

World War II

1939: On September 3rd, Britain declares war on Germany following the invasion of Poland. Churchill is appointed First Lord of the Admiralty, rejoining the war cabinet.

1940:

May 10th: Churchill becomes Prime Minister after Neville Chamberlain's resignation. He forms a coalition government.

May-June: Oversees the Dunkirk evacuation ("Operation Dynamo"), where over 338,000 Allied troops are rescued.

July-October: Leads Britain through the Battle of Britain, the first major military campaign fought entirely by air forces.

August-September: Endures The Blitz, the German bombing campaign against the UK, particularly London.

December: Initiates the "Lend-Lease" agreement with the United States, bolstering British military supplies.

1941: Successfully lobbies for increased American support, which culminates in the Atlantic Charter with President Franklin D. Roosevelt, outlining post-war world aims.

1942: Faces criticism at home for military setbacks in North Africa but sees a turn in fortunes with the victory at the Second Battle of El Alamein.

1943: Participates in strategic conferences with Allied leaders, including the Tehran Conference with Roosevelt and Joseph Stalin, planning the final strategy against the Axis powers.

1944: Plays a central role in planning and executing the D-Day invasion of Normandy, leading to the liberation of Western Europe from Nazi control. Continues to participate in key strategic meetings with Allied leaders, shaping the post-war world order.

1945: Celebrates Victory in Europe Day (VE Day) as Germany surrenders. Despite his wartime leadership, the Conservative Party loses the general election in July, and Churchill becomes Leader of the Opposition.

Post-War and Second Premiership

1951: Returns to office as Prime Minister after the Conservative victory in the October general election.

1953: Awarded the Nobel Prize in Literature; suffers a serious stroke that is kept secret from the public.

1955: Resigns as Prime Minister on April 5th due to declining health but remains an MP.

Final Years

1964: Retires from Parliament after serving as MP for Woodford since 1945.

1965: Passes away on January 24th; accorded a state funeral on January 30th, buried at St. Martin's Church, Bladon.

CONCLUSION

As we draw the curtains on "Winston Churchill: A Biography of the Bulldog of Britain," we have traversed the expanse of a life that was as tumultuous as it was triumphant, as fraught with failure as it was crowned with success. This concise, unofficial biography has endeavored to chart the course of Winston Churchill's journey, from his early days marked by a struggle for academic and social standing, through his military escapades that took him across continents, to his indelible impact on the political landscape of not just Britain but the world.

We began with Churchill's early life and education, a period that shaped the resilience and determination he would carry throughout his existence. His military beginnings and adventures across the globe were not just passages of valor but crucibles that forged his character and his understanding of the world's complexities. His entry into politics was met with both enthusiasm and skepticism, yet it set the stage for a career that would be defined by its highs and lows, its victories and defeats.

The Wilderness Years provided a reflective interlude, a time during which Churchill, though marginalized, honed his vision and voice, preparing for the storm he saw gathering on the horizon. With the outbreak of World War II, Churchill ascended to a role that seemed his destiny—to lead Britain through its darkest hour with a blend of defiance, determination, and eloquence that stirred a nation to stand firm against seemingly insurmountable odds.

In the postwar years and during his second premiership, we witnessed Churchill grappling with the realities of a world forever changed by war, striving to secure peace and stability in the face of new challenges. His final years, though marked by declining health, were illuminated by the recognition of his lifelong contributions to his country and humanity.

Beyond the political arena, we explored Churchill's life outside politics—his family, his hobbies, and his passion for painting and writing, which provided solace and satisfaction beyond the clamor of public life. His work as an author, which earned him the Nobel Prize in Literature, was highlighted, showcasing his prowess with the pen as well as the sword.

In concluding this biography, we are reminded of Churchill's complexity as a human being—his imperfections, his indefatigable spirit, and his enduring legacy. Through the chapters of his life, we have seen a man who was as much a product of his times as he was ahead of them, a leader whose words and deeds have left an indelible mark on the tapestry of history.

"Winston Churchill: A Biography of the Bulldog of Britain" has sought to provide a lens through which to view the life of a man who was, by all accounts, a colossal figure in the annals of the 20th century. His story is one of perseverance in the face of adversity, of leadership in times of crisis, and of an unwavering belief in the power of democracy and freedom. As we reflect on Churchill's life and legacy, we are reminded of the impact one individual can have on the course of history, and the enduring power of courage, conviction, and the capacity for renewal.

www.ingramcontent.com/pod-product-compliance
Lightning Source LLC
Chambersburg PA
CBHW070939120626
46546CB00004B/1477